# Play & Praise

**VOLUME 2**

## A PRESCHOOL MADE FOR PRAISE

Companion Products:

**Cassette Leader's Guide** 0-6330-1211-4
(Contains teaching materials, video, listening cassette, split-track accompaniment cassette, piano accompaniments)

**CD Leader's Guide** 0-6330-0767-6
(Contains teaching materials, video, listening CD, split-track accompaniment CD, piano accompaniments)

**Listening Cassette** 0-6330-0768-4
(available at a reduced price when bought in quantities of 10 or more)

**Listening CD** 0-6330-0769-2
(available at a reduced price when bought in quantities of 10 or more)

**Child's Activity Bag** 0-6330-0776-5
(contains an activity book, crayons, and a listening cassette)

**Cassette Promo Pak** 0-6330-0777-3

**CD Promo Pak** 0-6330-1233-5

Made FOR Praise

0-6330-0766-8

© Copyright 2000 MADE for PRAISE (a div. of LMM), Nashville, TN 37234.

All Scripture quotations are from the Holy Bible, New International Version
© 1973, 1978, 1984 International Bible Society, unless otherwise noted.

# Obedient Bee

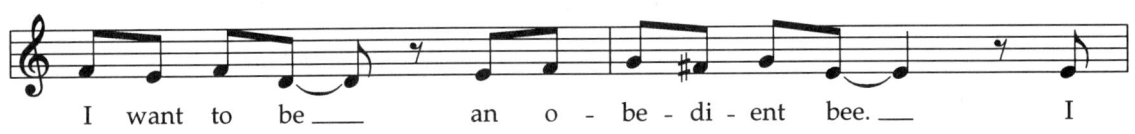

Words and Music by
PAM NOEL
Arranged by C. Barny Robertson

**Playful** (♩ = ca. 112)

O-be-di-ent bee, that's what I want to be. Yes, I want to be an o-be-di-ent bee. I want to be good, just like I should. Yes, I want to be an o-be-di-ent bee. Buzz, buzz, I want to be, buzz, buzz, buzz, an o-be-di-ent bee. I want to be good, just like I should. Yes, I want to be an o-be-di-ent bee.

© Copyright 2000 Broadman Press (SESAC).
Distributed by MADE for PRAISE (div. of LMM), Nashville, TN 37234.

# Obedient Bee

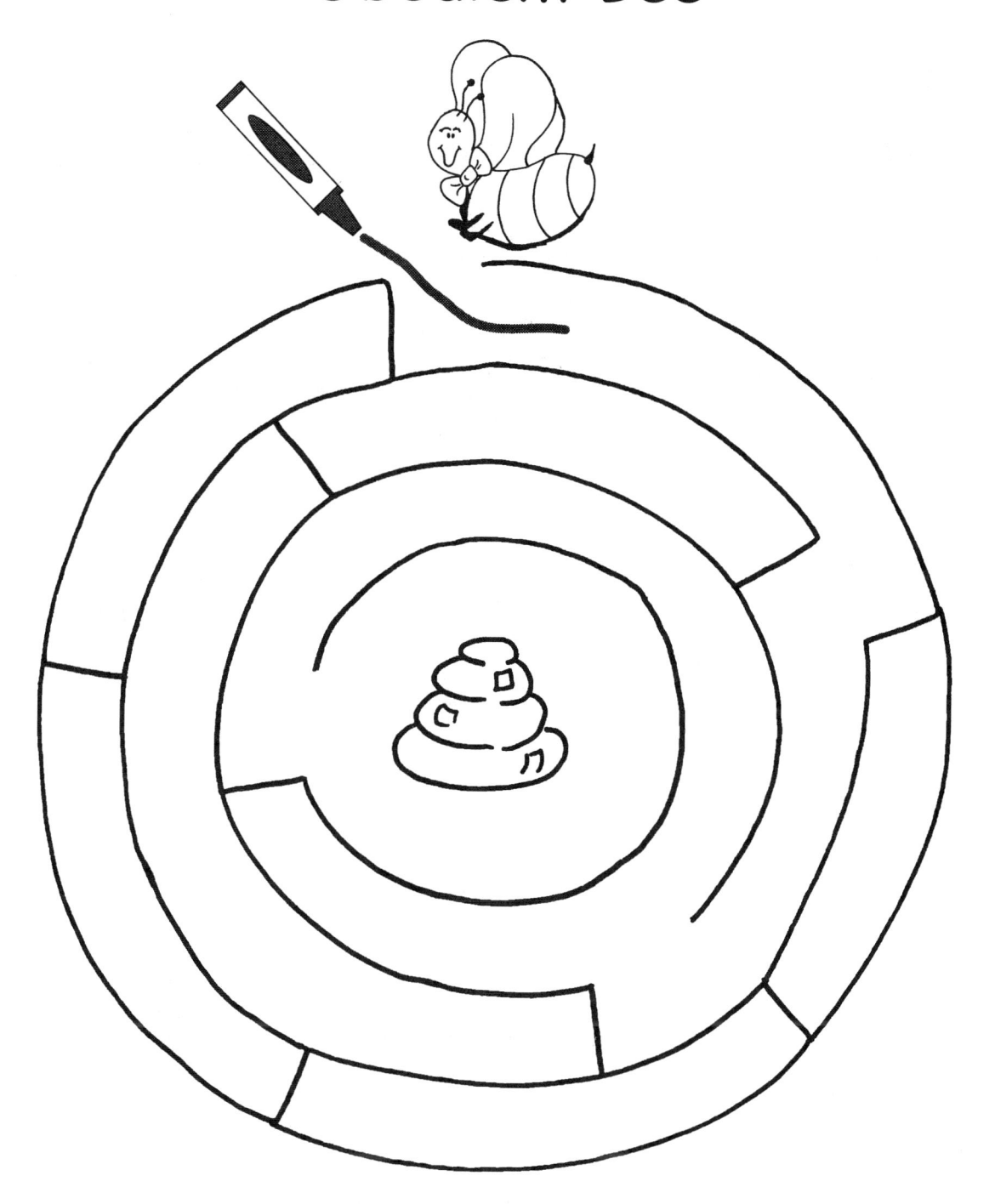

Help Obedient Bee buzz to his beehive so he can do his work!

# Three Little Bumblebees

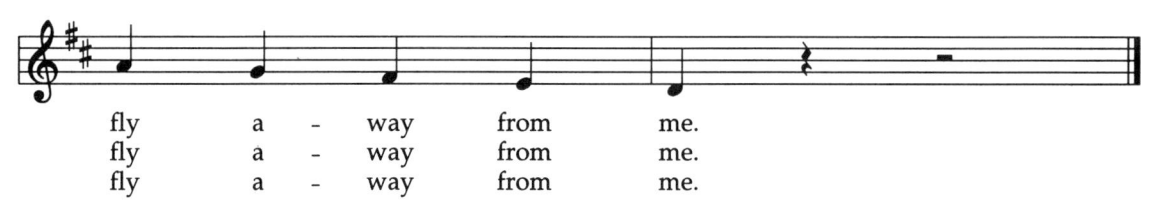

Words and Music by
ANITA WAGONER
Arranged by C. Barny Robertson

**Fun shuffle** (♩ = ca. 108)

*mf*

1. _____ Three little bumblebees flying all around my knees,
2. There were two little bumblebees flying all around my knees,
3. There was one little bumblebee flying all around my knees,

Mommy said if I'd be still they wouldn't bite me. So I
Mommy said if I'd be still they wouldn't bite me. So I
Mommy said if I'd be still he wouldn't bite me. So I

sat so silently and watched one little bee
sat so silently and watched one little bee
sat so silently and watched one little bee

fly away from me.
fly away from me.
fly away from me.

I'm so glad that I listened obediently
'cause those bees did not sting me.

*(spoken):* Mommy was right!

© Copyright 2000 Broadman Press (SESAC).
Distributed by MADE for PRAISE (a div. of LMM), Nashville, TN 37234.

# Three Little Bumblebees

Connect the dots to make a beehive for the buzzing bumblebees. Color the picture.

# Keep His Commandments

Words and Music by
RUTH ELAINE SCHRAM
Arranged by C. Barny Robertson

With a strong beat (♩ = ca. 80)

1. Keep His com - mand - ments,
2. Je - sus will help us

mem - o - rize the Word of God.
un - der - stand His prom - is - es.

Keep His com - mand - ments,
Nev - er for - get them,

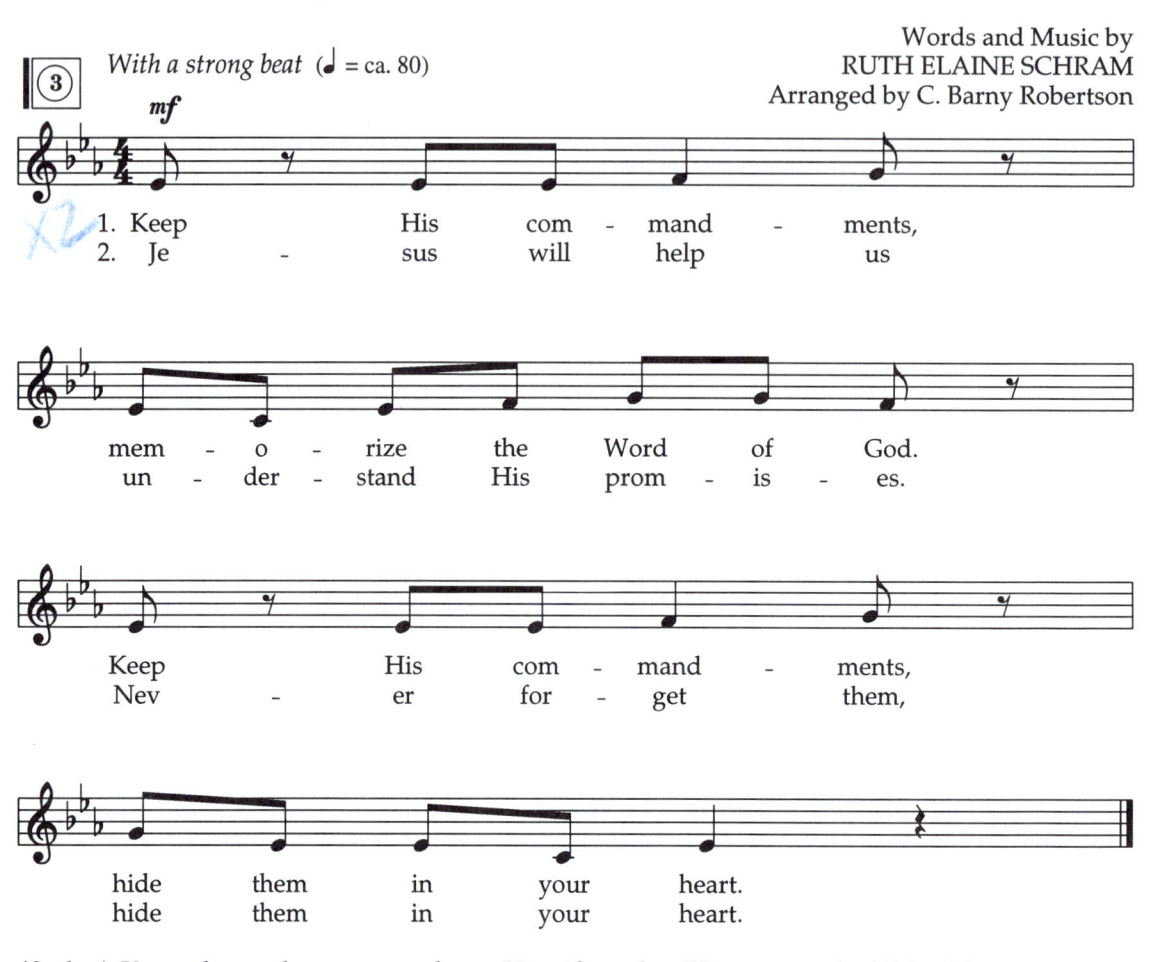

hide them in your heart.
hide them in your heart.

(Spoken): Know that we have come to know Him, if we obey His commands. 1 John 2:3

© Copyright 2000 Van Ness Press, Inc. (ASCAP).
Distributed by MADE for PRAISE (a div. of LMM), Nashville, TN 37234.

# Keep His Commandments

Color the ♡ red
Color the ☆ blue

# Do the Right Thing / Trust and Obey

Words and Music by
ROBERT NELSON
Arranged by C. Barny Robertson

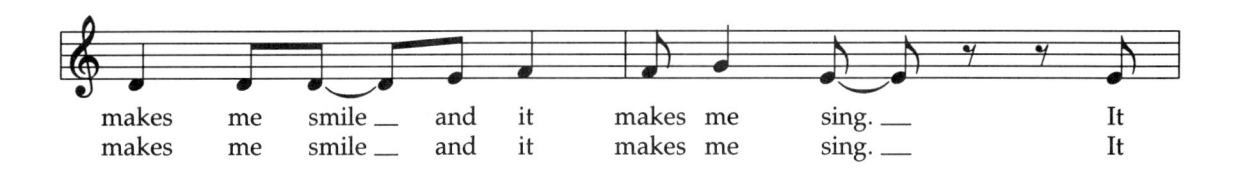

[4] Light calypso beat (♩ = ca. 108)

1. It makes me hap-py to do the right thing,— It makes me smile and it makes me sing.— It shows I be-long to Je-sus, my King.— It makes me hap-py to do the right thing.—

2. It makes me hap-py to say the right thing,— It makes me smile and it makes me sing.— It shows I be-long to Je-sus, my King.— It makes me hap-py to say the right thing.—

*Trust and obey, For there's no other way,
To be happy in Jesus, But to trust and obey.

*"Trust and Obey," Words by JOHN H. SAMMIS; Music by DANIEL B. TOWNER.

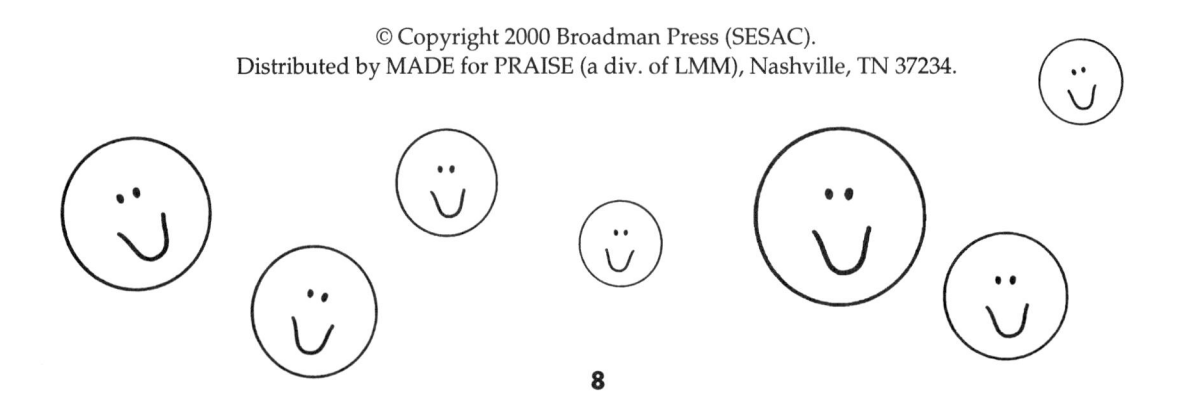

© Copyright 2000 Broadman Press (SESAC).
Distributed by MADE for PRAISE (a div. of LMM), Nashville, TN 37234.

# Do the Right Thing

Draw a ☺ by each picture
if the children are doing the right thing.

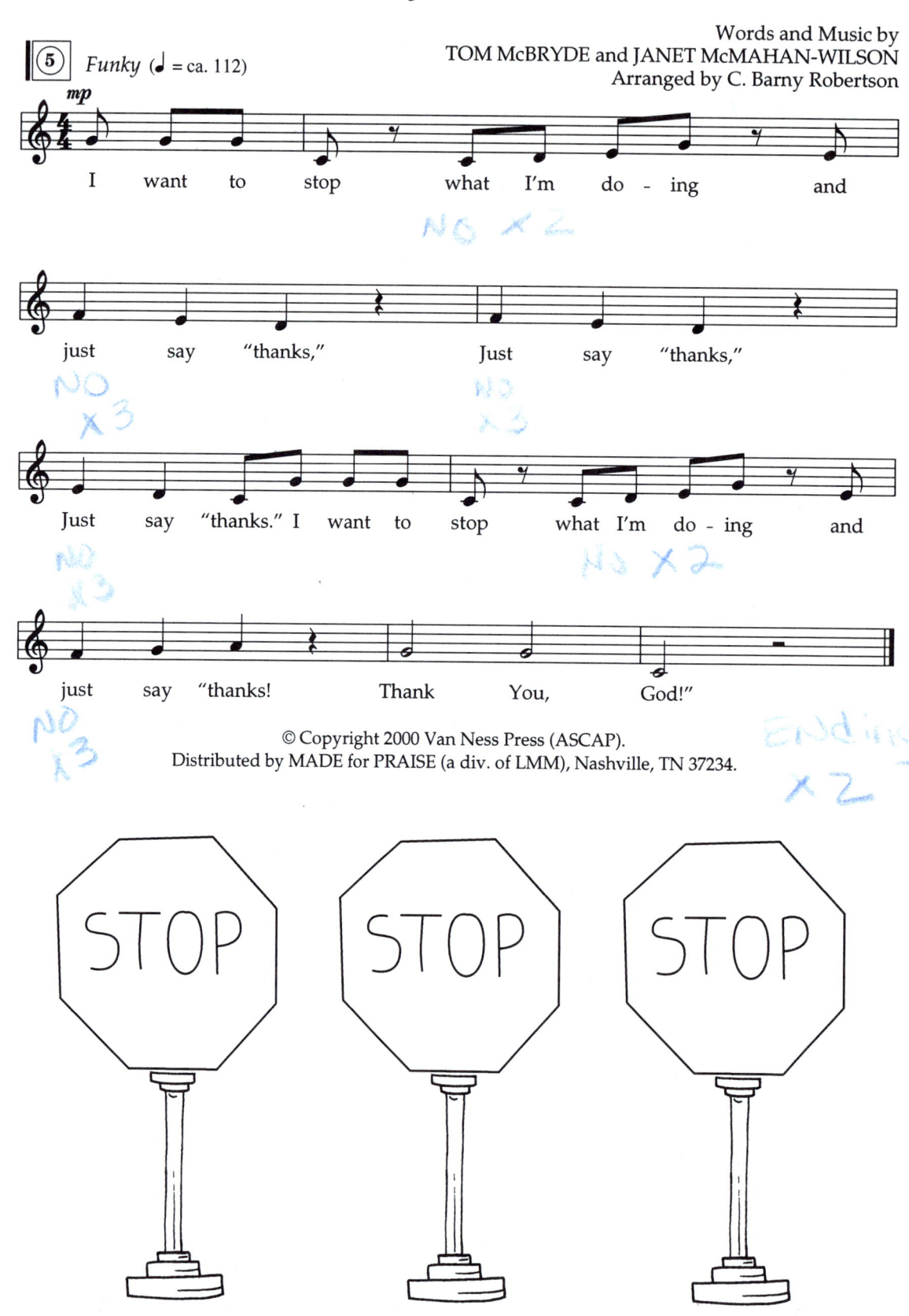

# Just Say "Thanks"

**Words and Music by
TOM McBRYDE and JANET McMAHAN-WILSON
Arranged by C. Barny Robertson**

*Funky* (♩ = ca. 112)

I want to stop what I'm doing and just say "thanks," Just say "thanks," Just say "thanks." I want to stop what I'm doing and just say "thanks! Thank You, God!"

© Copyright 2000 Van Ness Press (ASCAP).
Distributed by MADE for PRAISE (a div. of LMM), Nashville, TN 37234.

# Just Say "Thanks"

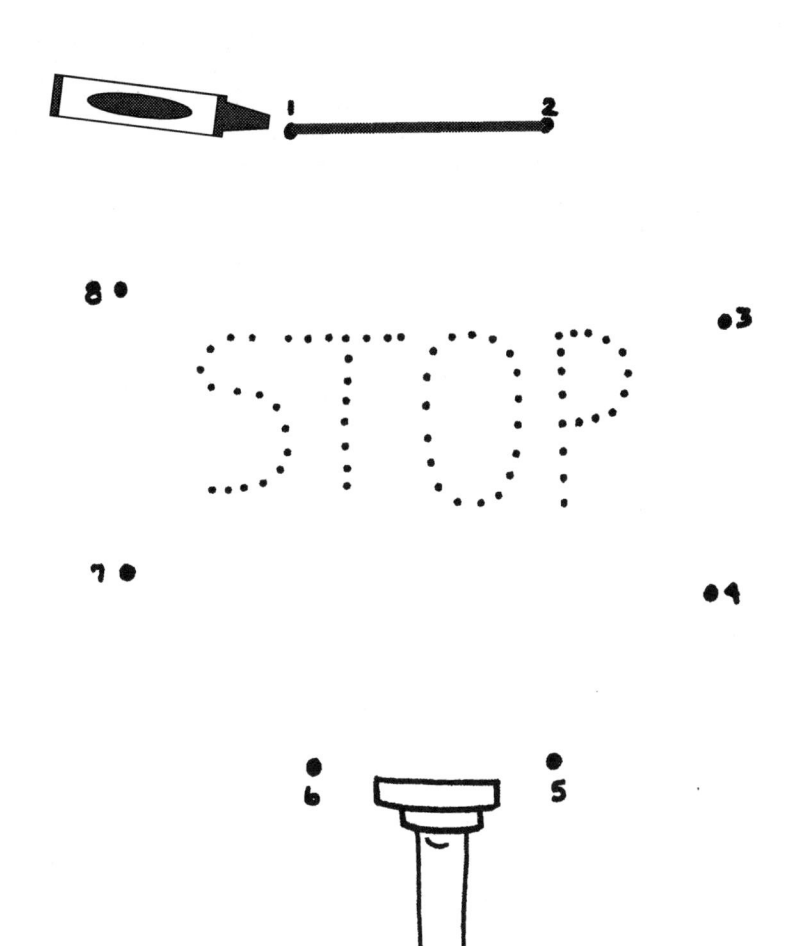

**STOP**

Connect the dots. Trace the letters.
Color the sign.

# Thank You, Lord, for My Two Hands

*Light and detached* (♩ = ca. 152)

Words and Music by
CATHY SPURR and DEBBIE McNEIL
Arranged by C. Barny Robertson

*mf*

1. Thank You, Lord, for my two hands. — I can clap with my two hands.
2. Thank You, Lord, for my two feet. — I can march with my two feet.
3. Thank You, Lord, for my two lips. I'll blow a kiss with my two lips.

Thank You, Lord, for my two hands. — I can clap a-long and thank You.
Thank You, Lord, for my two feet. — I can march a-long and thank You.
Thank You, Lord, for my two lips. I'll blow a kiss and just say, "Thank You."

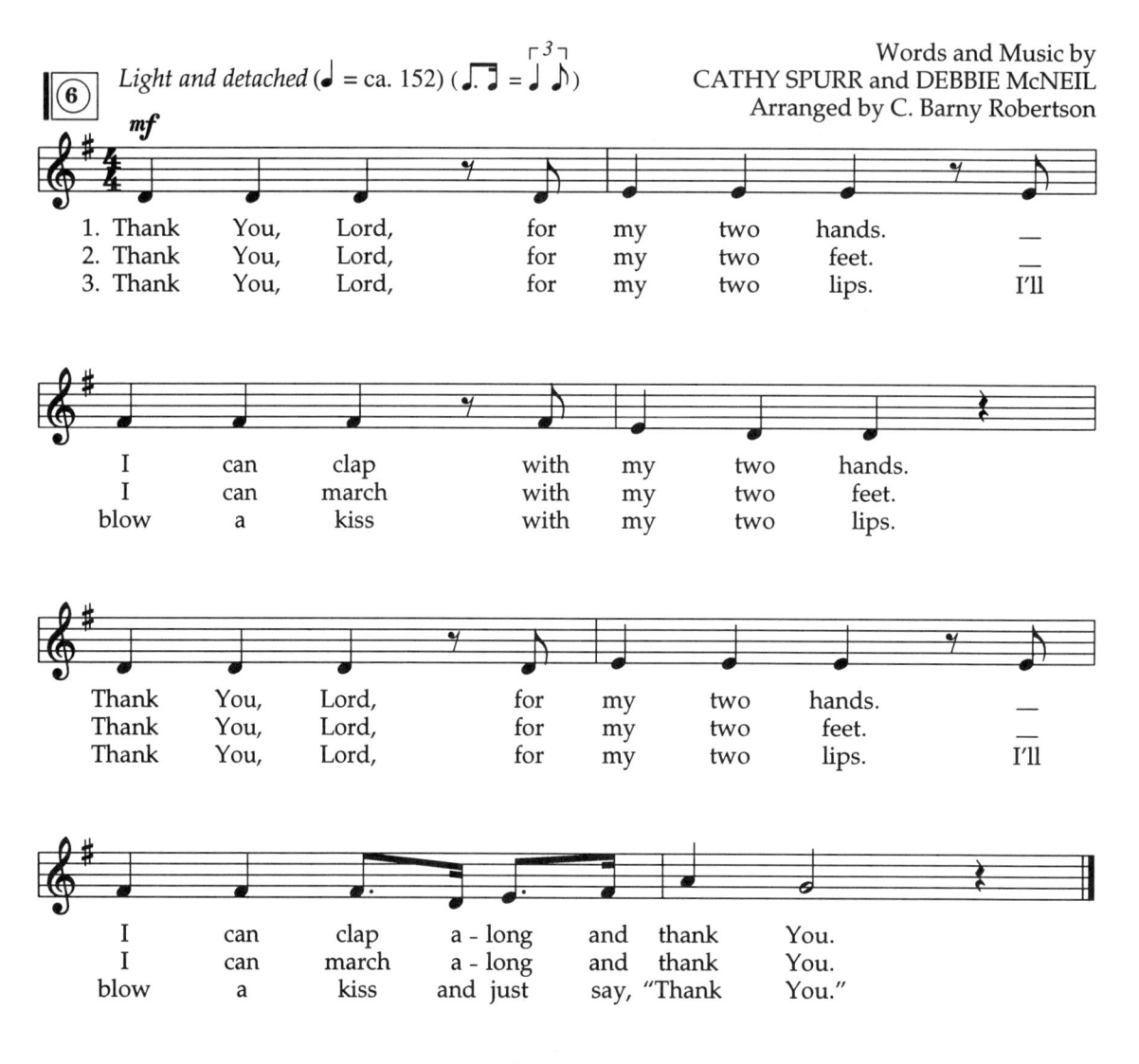

© Copyright 2000 Parbar Music.
All rights reserved. Used by permission.

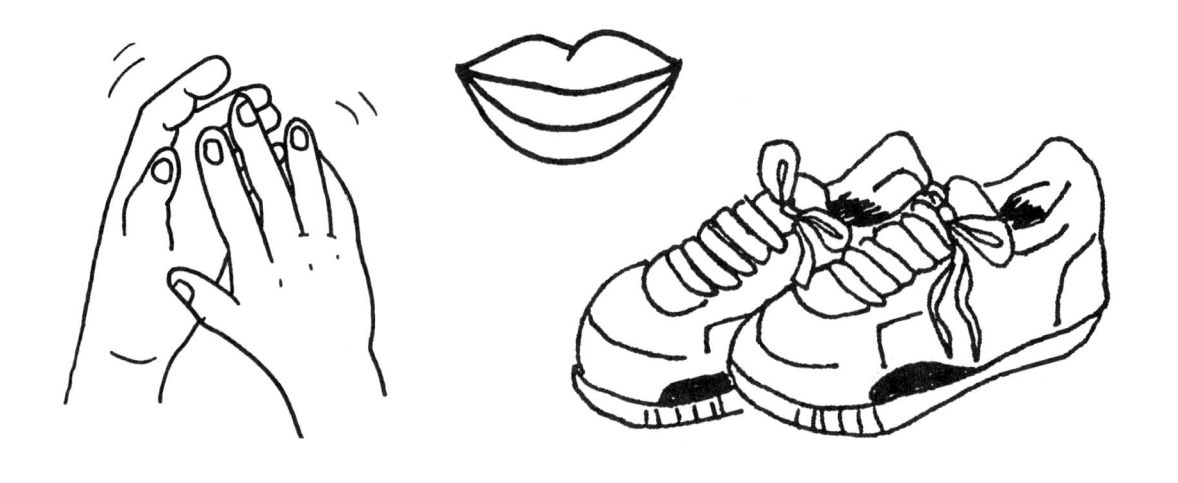

# Thank You, Lord, for My Two Hands

Finish the picture.
Draw the things that are missing

Thank You, Lord, for my _____    How many?

Thank You, Lord, for my _____    How many?

Thank You, Lord, for my _____    How many?

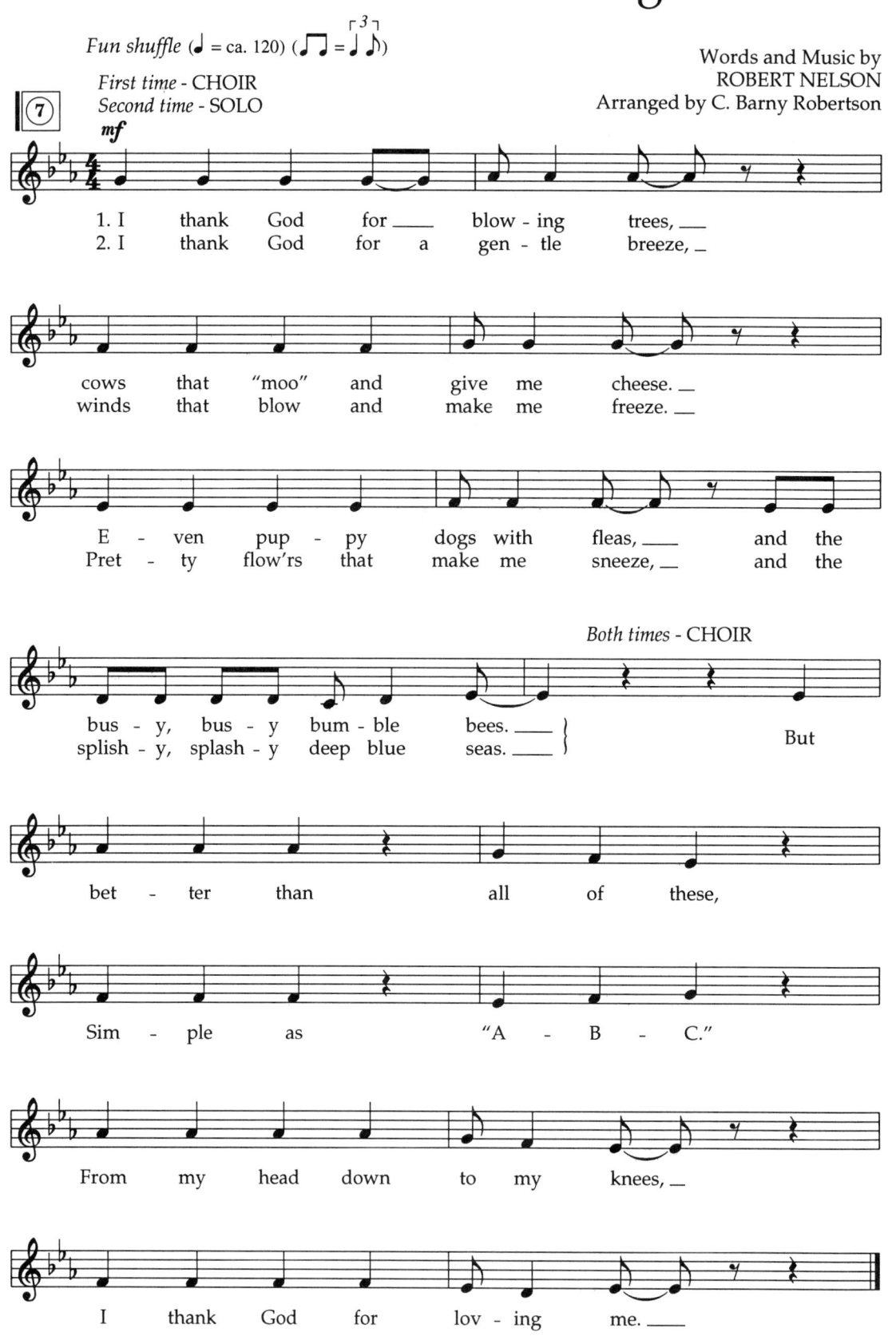

# I Thank God for Loving Me

*Fun shuffle* (♩ = ca. 120)

First time - CHOIR
Second time - SOLO

Words and Music by
ROBERT NELSON
Arranged by C. Barny Robertson

1. I thank God for blow-ing trees, cows that "moo" and give me cheese. E-ven pup-py dogs with fleas, and the bus-y, bus-y bum-ble bees.

2. I thank God for a gen-tle breeze, winds that blow and make me freeze. Pret-ty flow'rs that make me sneeze, and the splish-y, splash-y deep blue seas.

*Both times - CHOIR*

But bet-ter than all of these, Sim-ple as "A - B - C." From my head down to my knees, I thank God for lov-ing me.

© Copyright 2000 Broadman Press (SESAC).
Distributed by MADE for PRAISE (a div. of LMM), Nashville, TN 37234.

# I Thank God for Loving Me

Draw a string from each balloon
to a blessing God gives us.
Color the pictures.

# Thank You, Lord

Words and Music by
TERESA MOSHELL
Arranged by C. Barny Robertson

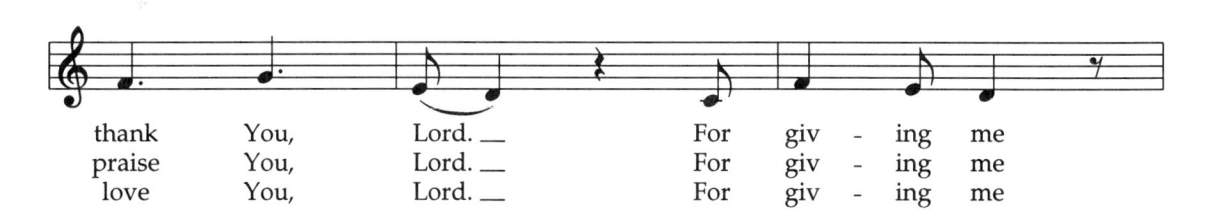

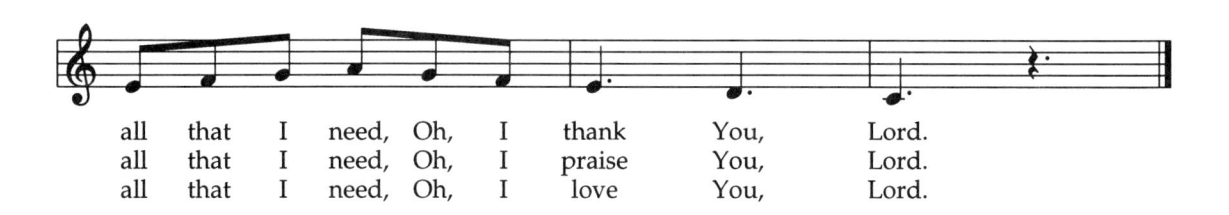

*Flowing* (♩. = ca. 63)
*mp*

1. Thank You, Lord, Oh, how I thank You, Lord. __ Thank You, Lord, Oh, how I thank You, Lord. __ For giv-ing me all that I need, Oh, I thank You, Lord.
2. Praise You, Lord, Oh, how I praise You, Lord. __ Praise You, Lord, Oh, how I praise You, Lord. __ For giv-ing me all that I need, Oh, I praise You, Lord.
3. Love You, Lord, Oh, how I love You, Lord. __ Love You, Lord, Oh, how I love You, Lord. __ For giv-ing me all that I need, Oh, I love You, Lord.

© Copyright 2000 Centergy Music/BMI (admin. by ICG).
All rights reserved. Used by permission.

# Thank You, Lord

Put a 🍃 around the plants.

Put a 🐷 around the animals.

# Great Big Praise

Words and Music by
JOHN CHISUM and NANCY GORDON
Arranged by C. Barny Robertson

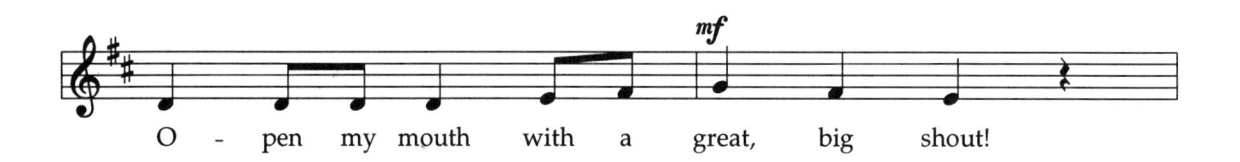

*Baroque feel* (♩ = ca. 138)

My lit-tle sound makes a great, big praise.

Hal - le - lu, hal - le - lu.

O - pen my mouth with a great, big shout!

Hal - le - lu - jah, Lord.

Hallelujah, I will sing.
Hallelujah, Christ is King.
My little sound makes a great big praise!
Hallelujah, Lord.

© Copyright 1999 Mother's Heart Music and ThreeFold Amen/ASCAP.
c/o ROM Administration, 8315 Twin Lakes Dr., Mobile, AL 36695.

# Great Big Praise

◯ the children with a tall open mouth.

✗ the children with a closed mouth.

# Building Lives Together

Words and Music by
ANITA WAGONER
Arranged by C. Barny Robertson

*March feel* (♩ = ca. 108)

Hi, ho, here we go, we're build-ing lives to-geth-er. Hi, ho, here we go, we're learn-ing of God's Word.

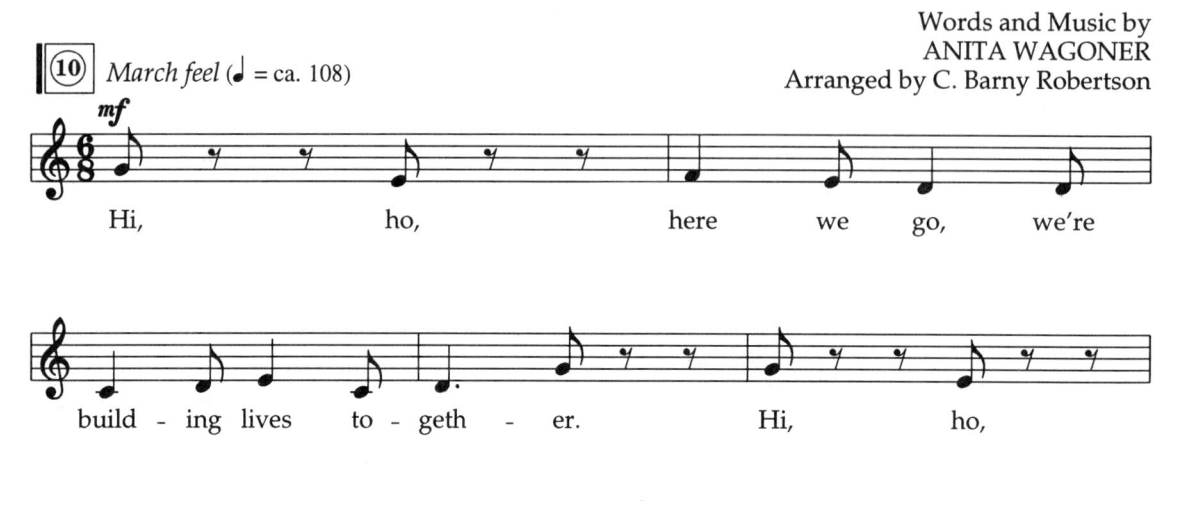

Build the floor on the Word of God,
Build the walls on His love.
Cover it all with a roof of prayer,
God will always be there.

© Copyright 2000 Broadman Press (SESAC).
Distributed by MADE for PRAISE (a div. of LMM), Nashville, TN 37234.

# Building Lives Together

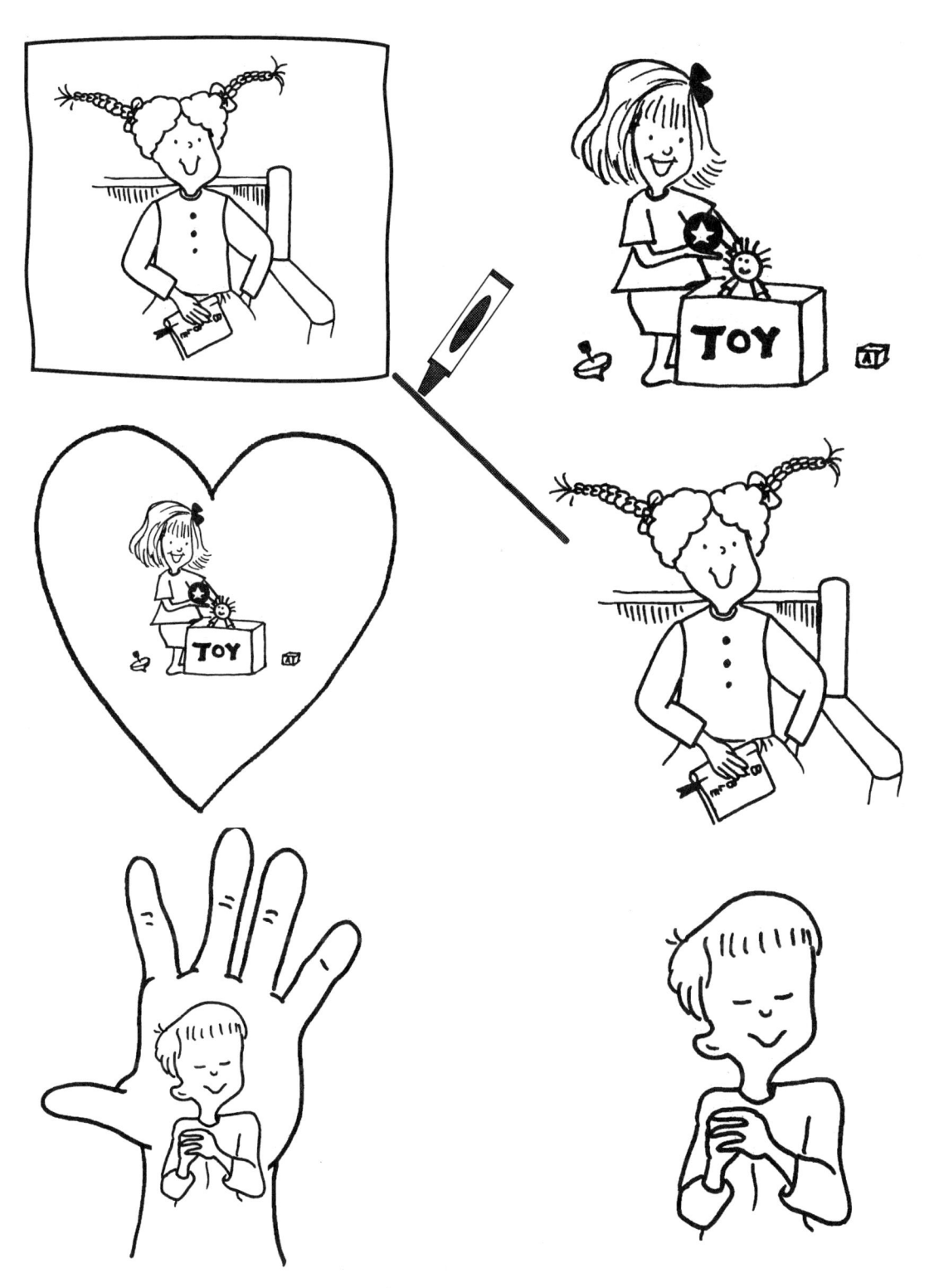

Match the pictures.

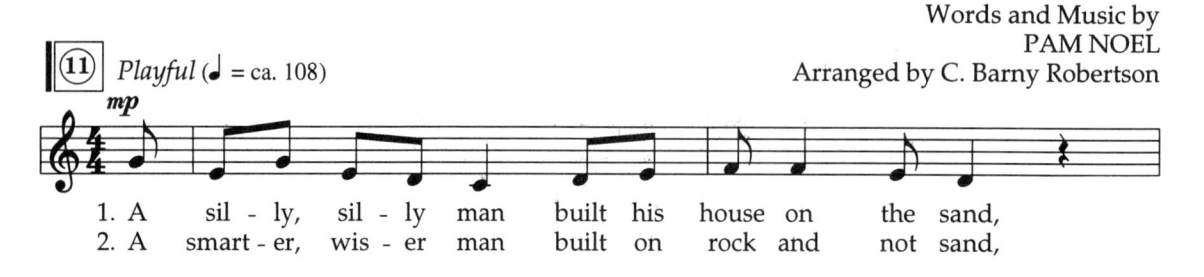

# House on the Sand

Words and Music by
PAM NOEL
Arranged by C. Barny Robertson

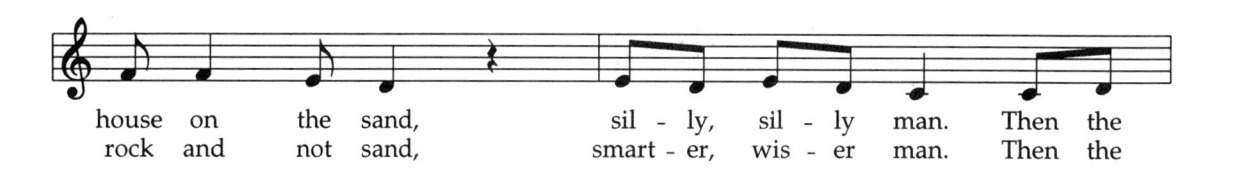

Playful (♩ = ca. 108)

*mp*

1. A sil-ly, sil-ly man built his house on the sand,
2. A smart-er, wis-er man built on rock and not sand,

house on the sand, sil-ly, sil-ly man. Then the
rock and not sand, smart-er, wis-er man. Then the

wind be-gan to blow a-round and 'round and 'round, It
wind be-gan to blow a-round and 'round and 'round, But

tossed the house up in the sky and plopped it on the ground!
that old house built on the rock stood firm-ly on the ground!

© Copyright 2000 Broadman Press (SESAC).
Distributed by MADE for PRAISE (a div. of LMM), Nashville, TN 37234.

# House on the Sand

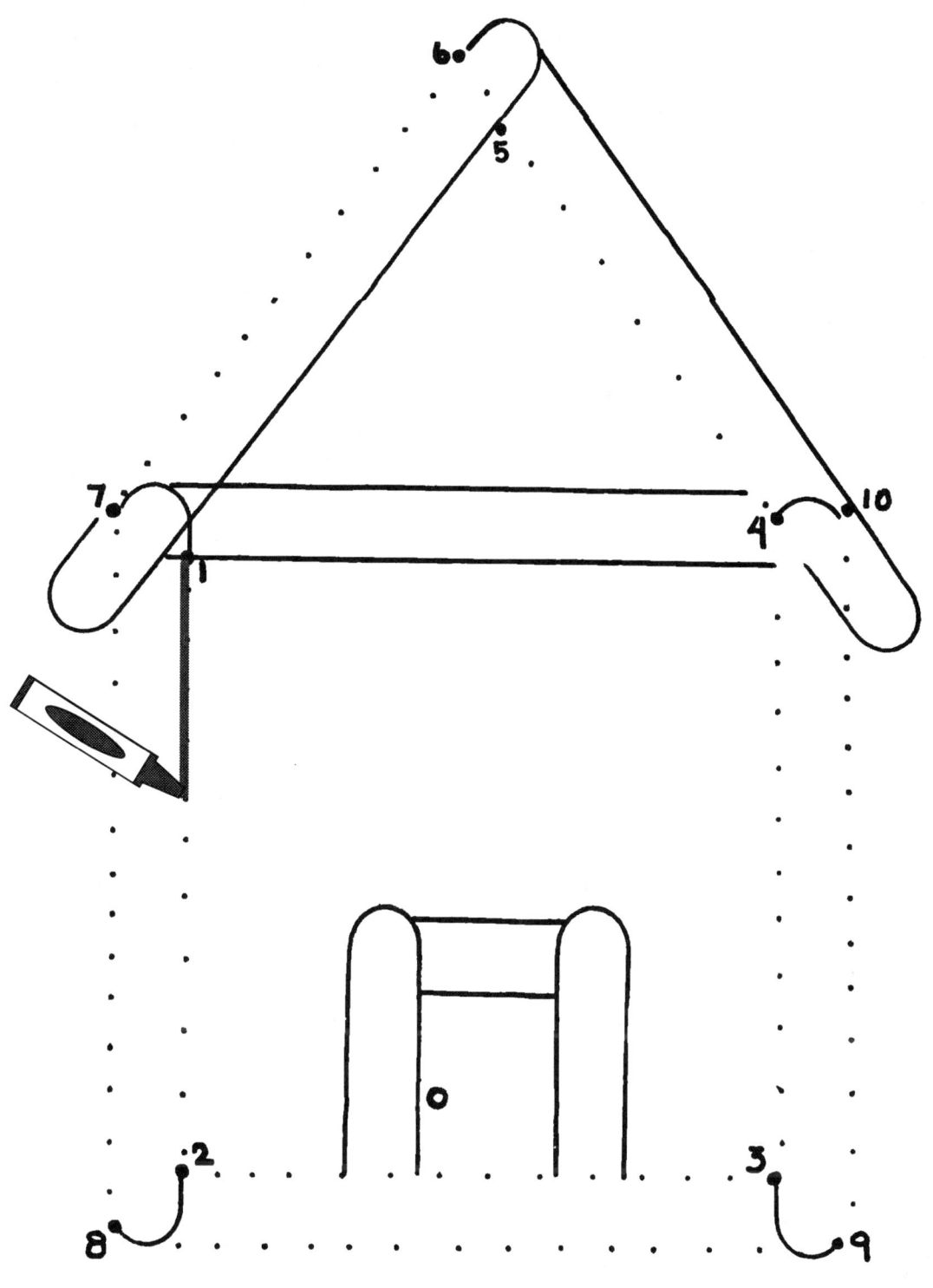

Connect all of the dots.
Color your house.

# Built on the Word

Words and Music by
KATHIE HILL
Arranged by C. Barny Robertson

Shuffle (♩ = ca. 112)

1. Built on the Word, um hmm. Built on the Word, um hmm. Built on God's Word strong and true, Add some love and pray-ing, too.
2. Built on His love, um hmm. Built on His love, um hmm. Built on God's Word strong and true, Add some love and pray-ing, too.
3. Built on prayer, um hmm. Built on prayer, um hmm. Built on God's Word strong and true, Add some love and pray-ing too.

4. Built on the Word, um hmm.
Built on the Word, um hmm.
Built on God's word strong and true,
Add some love and praying, too.

© Copyright 1995, this arr. 2000, Van Ness Press, Inc. (ASCAP).
Distributed by MADE for PRAISE (a div. of LMM), Nashville, TN 37234.

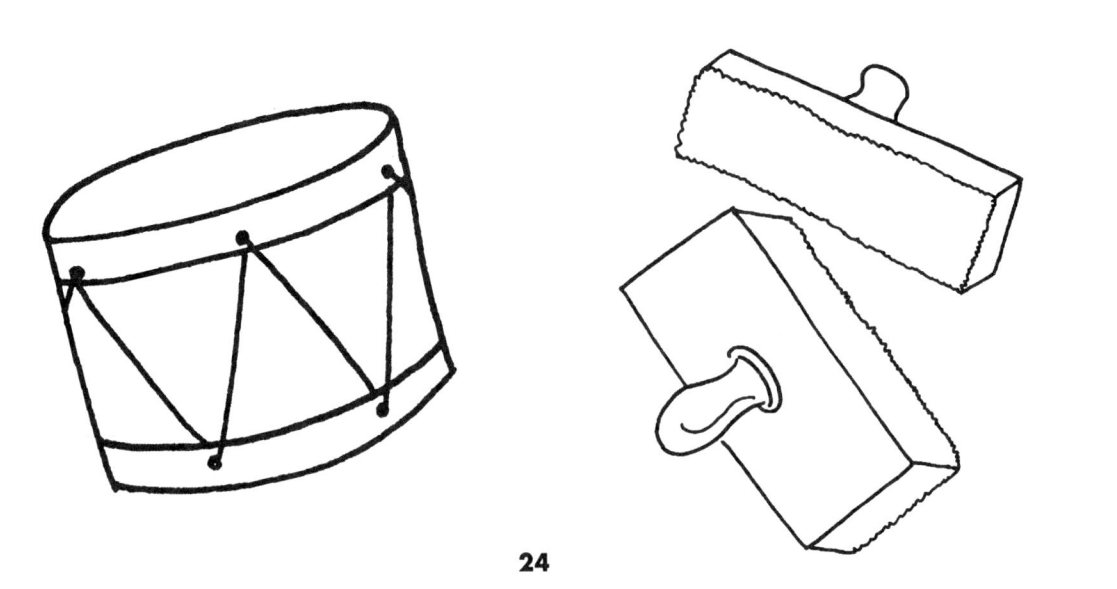

# Built on the Word

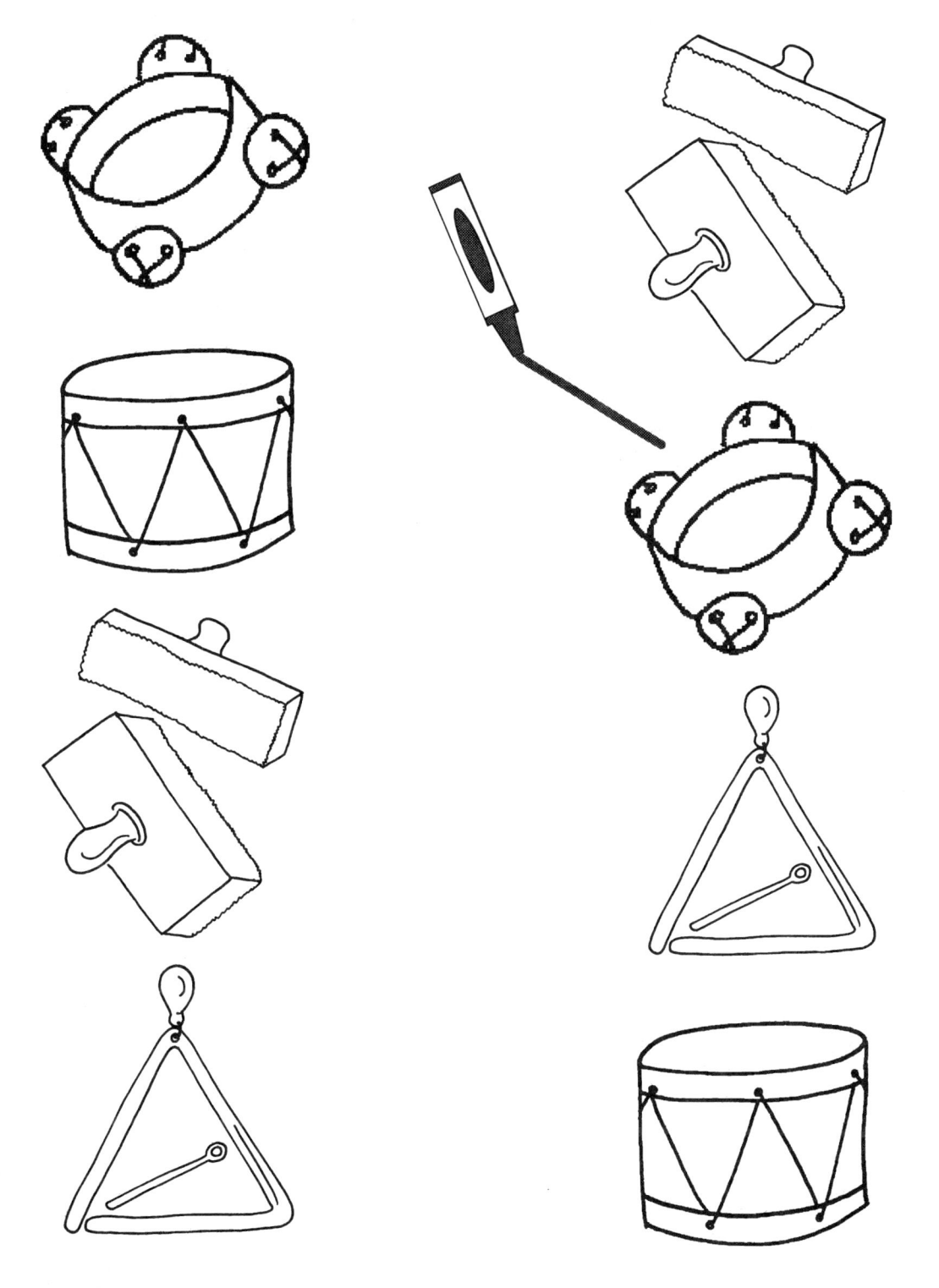

Match the instruments you could play to "Built on the Word."

25

# Building Blocks

Words and Music by
ANITA WAGONER
Arranged by C. Barny Robertson

Shuffle (♩ = ca. 116)

1. Ev-'ry-bod-y us-es build-ing blocks to make their hous-es strong. Ev-'ry-bod-y us-es build-ing plans, So they won't build things wrong. Build with blocks, strong and firm. Us-ing things that we have learned. Build with blocks, strong and firm. We're build-ing on what we've learned.

2. Ev-'ry-bod-y us-es build-ing blocks to make their lives so strong. Ev-'ry-bod-y us-es build-ing plans, So they won't live life wrong. Build-ing lives strong and firm. Us-ing things that we have learned. Build-ing lives strong and firm. We're build-ing on what we've learned.

SPEAKER 1: I seek You with all my heart, do not let me stray from Your commands. Psalm 119:10
SPEAKER 2: Pray without ceasing. 1 Thessalonians 5:17 (KJV)
SPEAKER 3: Since God so loved us, we also ought to love one another. 1 John 4:11
SPEAKER 4: For no one can lay any foundation other than the one already laid, which is Jesus Christ. 1 Corinthians 3:11

© Copyright 2000 Broadman Press (SESAC).
Distributed by MADE for PRAISE (a div. of LMM), Nashville, TN 37234.

# Building Blocks

Finish the blocks and help Joash build the temple.

# I Belong to God

Words and Music by
LINDA L. WALKER
Arranged by C. Barny Robertson

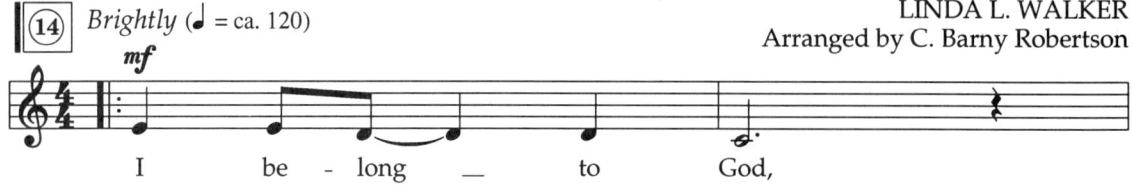

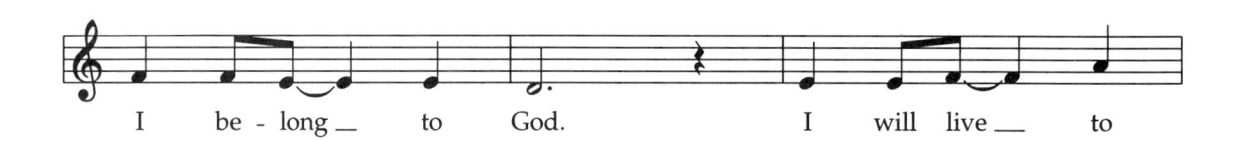

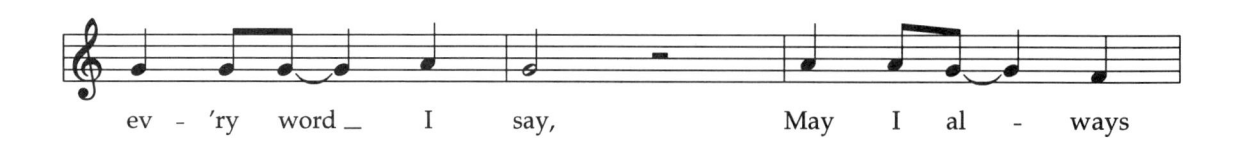

*Brightly* (♩ = ca. 120)

I be-long to God, I be-long to God. I will live to serve Him, for I be-long to God. Yes, I be-long to God. God.

**SOLO**

In ev-'ry-thing I do, with ev-'ry word I say, May I al-ways please You, Lord, yes, please You, Lord, I pray.

© Copyright 2000 Van Ness Press (ASCAP).
Distributed by MADE for PRAISE (a div. of LMM), Nashville, TN 37234.

# I Belong to God

I

God

Match the things that go together.

# Just Like Samuel

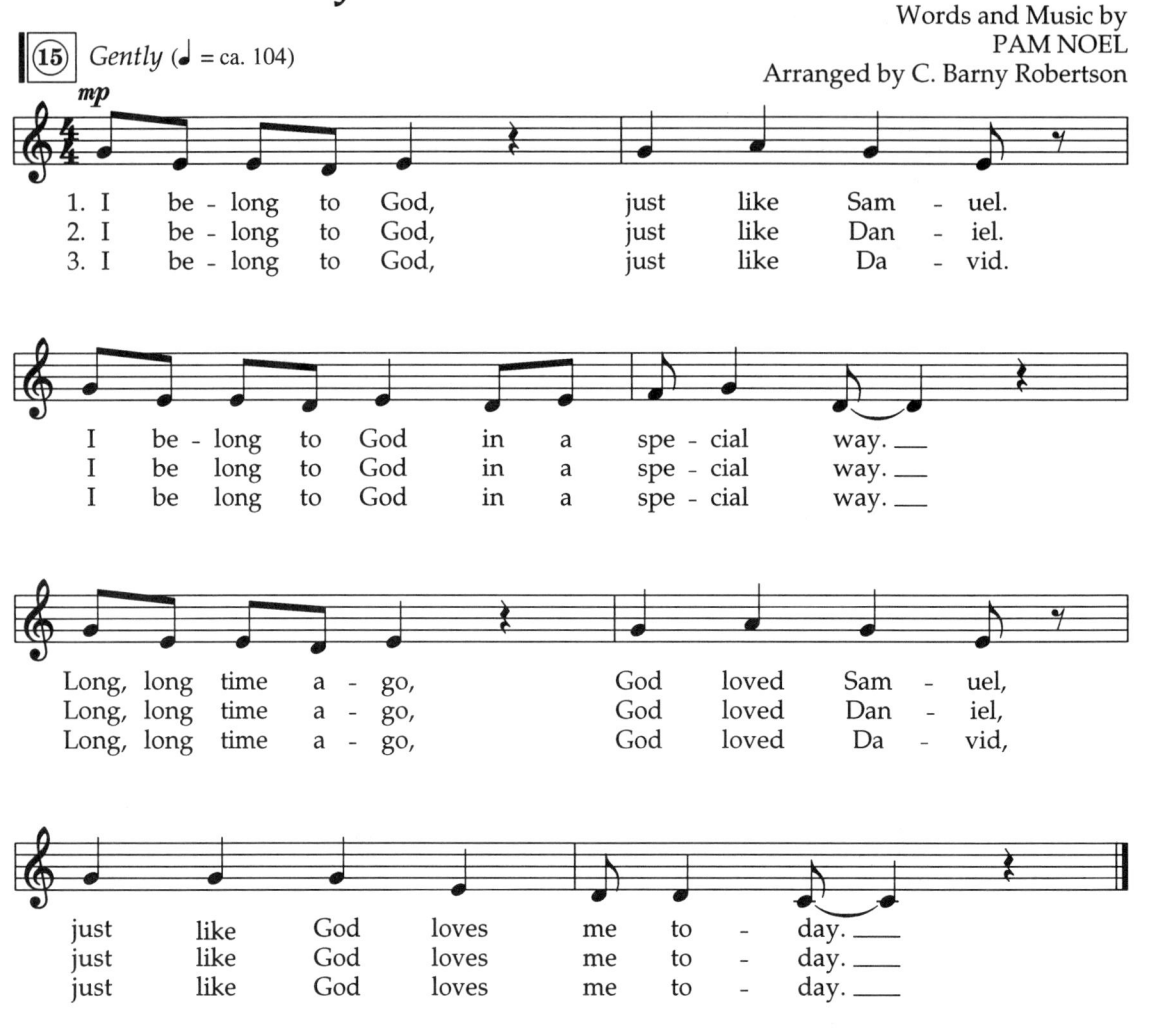

Words and Music by
PAM NOEL
Arranged by C. Barny Robertson

Gently (♩ = ca. 104)

1. I belong to God, just like Samuel.
2. I belong to God, just like Daniel.
3. I belong to God, just like David.

I belong to God in a special way.
I belong to God in a special way.
I belong to God in a special way.

Long, long time ago, God loved Samuel,
Long, long time ago, God loved Daniel,
Long, long time ago, God loved David,

just like God loves me today.
just like God loves me today.
just like God loves me today.

© Copyright 2000 Broadman Press (SESAC).
Distributed by MADE for PRAISE (a div. of LMM), Nashville, TN 37234.

# Just Like Samuel

Circle the one in each line
that is different.

# Thank You, God, for Loving Me

Words and Music by
PAM NOEL
Arranged by C. Barny Robertson

"Two" feel (♩ = ca. 126)

(16) *Sing first and third times*

Thank You, God, for lov - ing me. Thank You, God, for lov - ing me.

You are the King, who made ev - 'ry - thing, Thank You, God, for lov - ing me.

*Second time:* I will sing of the Lord's great love forever; with my mouth I will make Your faithfulness known through all generations. I will declare that Your love stands firm forever. Psalm 89:1-2

© Copyright 2000 Broadman Press (SESAC).
Distributed by MADE for PRAISE (div. of LMM), Nashville, TN 37234.

# Thank You, God, for Loving Me

Count the places that God is with you.
Color the pictures.

# Up Real High

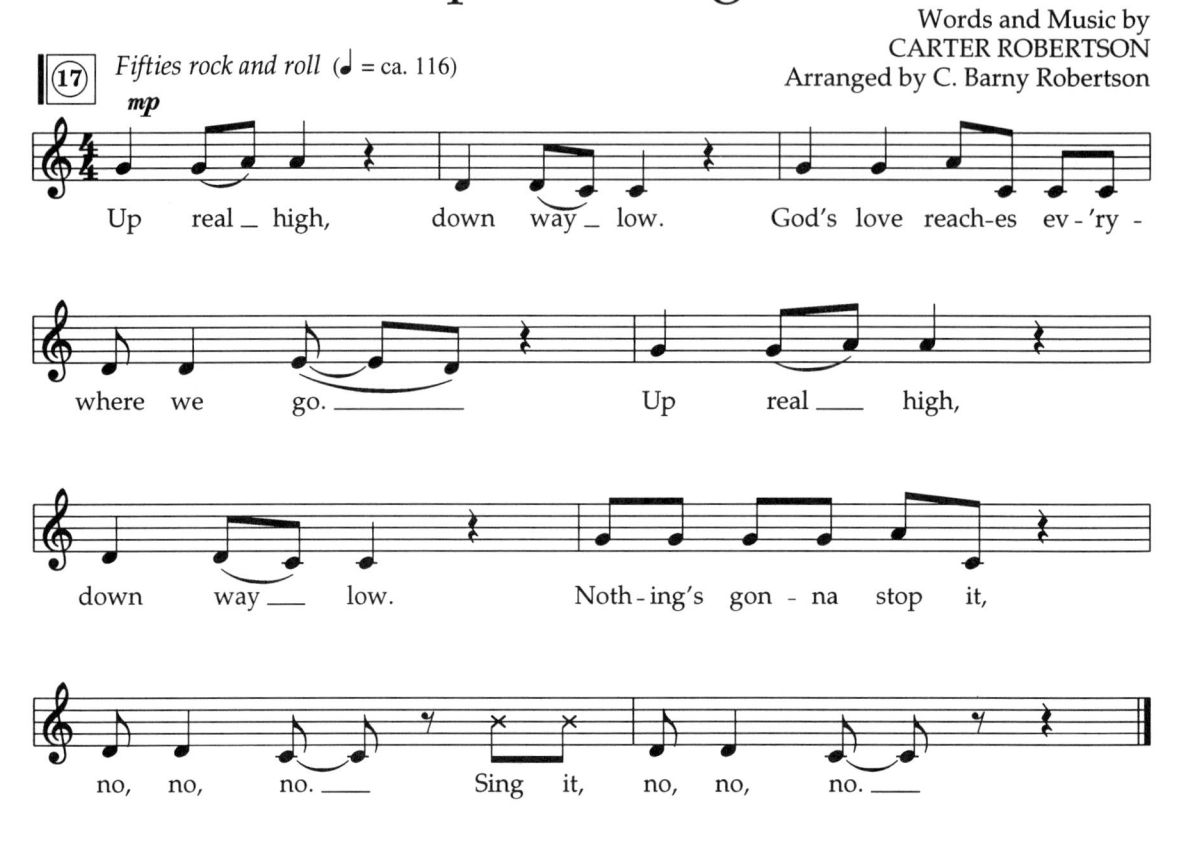

Words and Music by
CARTER ROBERTSON
Arranged by C. Barny Robertson

*Fifties rock and roll* (♩ = ca. 116)

Up real high, down way low. God's love reach-es ev-'ry-where we go. Up real high, down way low. Noth-ing's gon-na stop it, no, no, no. Sing it, no, no, no.

Who's that walking by your side.
Jesus, oh, Jesus.
Who's never gonna leave you, never say goodbye.
Jesus, oh, Jesus.

Who's the King, the Lord of all.
Jesus, oh, Jesus.
So don't give up, keep a-walking tall with
Jesus, oh, Jesus.

© Copyright 2000 McKinney Music, Inc. (BMI).
Distributed by MADE for PRAISE (a div. of LMM), Nashville, TN 37234.

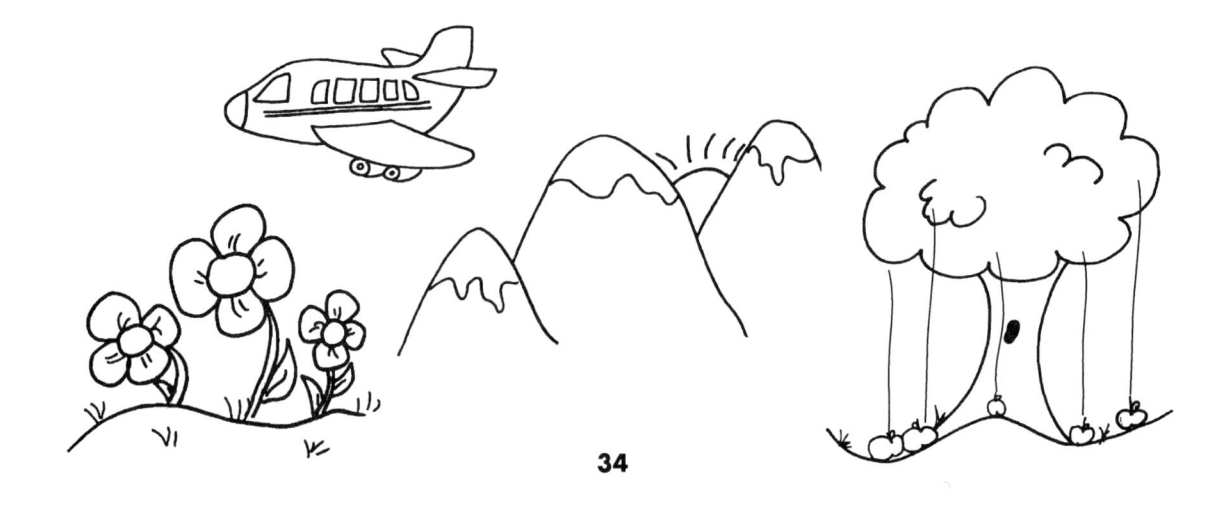

# Everywhere-God is There!

The high things.

The low things.

# I Can Talk to God

*Words and Music by*
**BILL F. LEACH and SAM SANDERS**
*Arranged by C. Barny Robertson*

(18) *Bright swing* (♩ = ca. 112) (♫ = ♩♪)

*mf*

1. I can talk to God,
2. I can talk to God,

an-y-where I am:
an-y-time of day:

Home or church or school or play, He
Ear-ly morn-ing, late at night, He

lis-tens when I pray.
hears each word I say.

© Copyright 2000 Van Ness Press (ASCAP).
Distributed by **MADE for PRAISE** (a div. of LMM), Nashville, TN 37234.

# I Can Talk to God

Follow the maze to get home!
We can talk to God anywhere we go!

# Walk with Jesus

Words and Music by
LINDA L. WALKER
Arranged by C. Barny Robertson

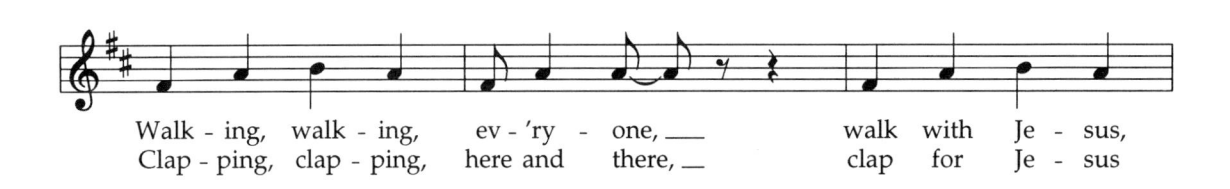

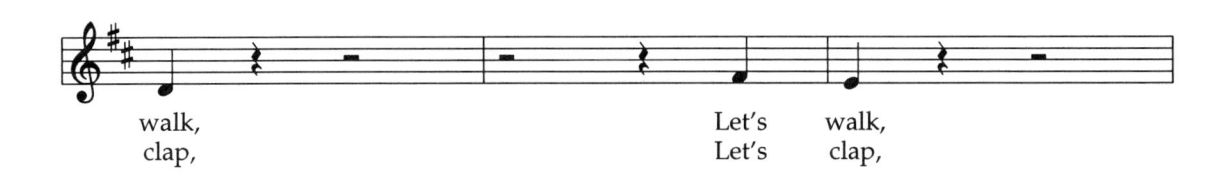

With drive (♩ = ca. 120)
*mf*

1. Walk - ing, walk - ing, come with me, ___
2. Clap - ping, clap - ping, up and down, ___

Walk with Je - sus, one, two, three. ___
Clap for Je - sus all a - round. ___

Walk - ing, walk - ing, ev - 'ry - one, ___ walk with Je - sus,
Clap - ping, clap - ping, here and there, ___ clap for Je - sus

it's so fun. ___ Let's walk, Let's
ev - 'ry - where. ___ Let's clap, Let's

walk, Let's walk,
clap, Let's clap,

Let's walk.
Let's clap.

© Copyright 2000 Van Ness Press (ASCAP).
Distributed by MADE for PRAISE (a div. of LMM), Nashville, TN 37234.

# Walk with Jesus

Match the shoes each person uses to walk with Jesus.

# Jesus, You Are Wonderful

Words and Music by
AMY SUSAN FOSTER
Arranged by C. Barny Robertson

Je - sus, You are won - der - ful.
Je - sus, You are won - der - ful. I will
count my bless - ings ev - 'ry day,
Je - sus, You're won - der - ful to me.

1. Ev'ry morning when I wake up,
   Jesus, You're wonderful to me.
   You make the birds sing and the sun come up,
   Jesus, You're wonderful to me.

2. You make the rain fall and flowers grow,
   Jesus, You're wonderful to me.
   You gave me a fam'ly that loves me so,
   Jesus, You're wonderful to me.

© Copyright 2000 Centergy Music/BMI (admin. by ICG).
All rights reserved. Used by permission.

# Jesus, You are Wonderful

X out the one that is different.

Help Buzzy find his hive.

Color Miss Honey.

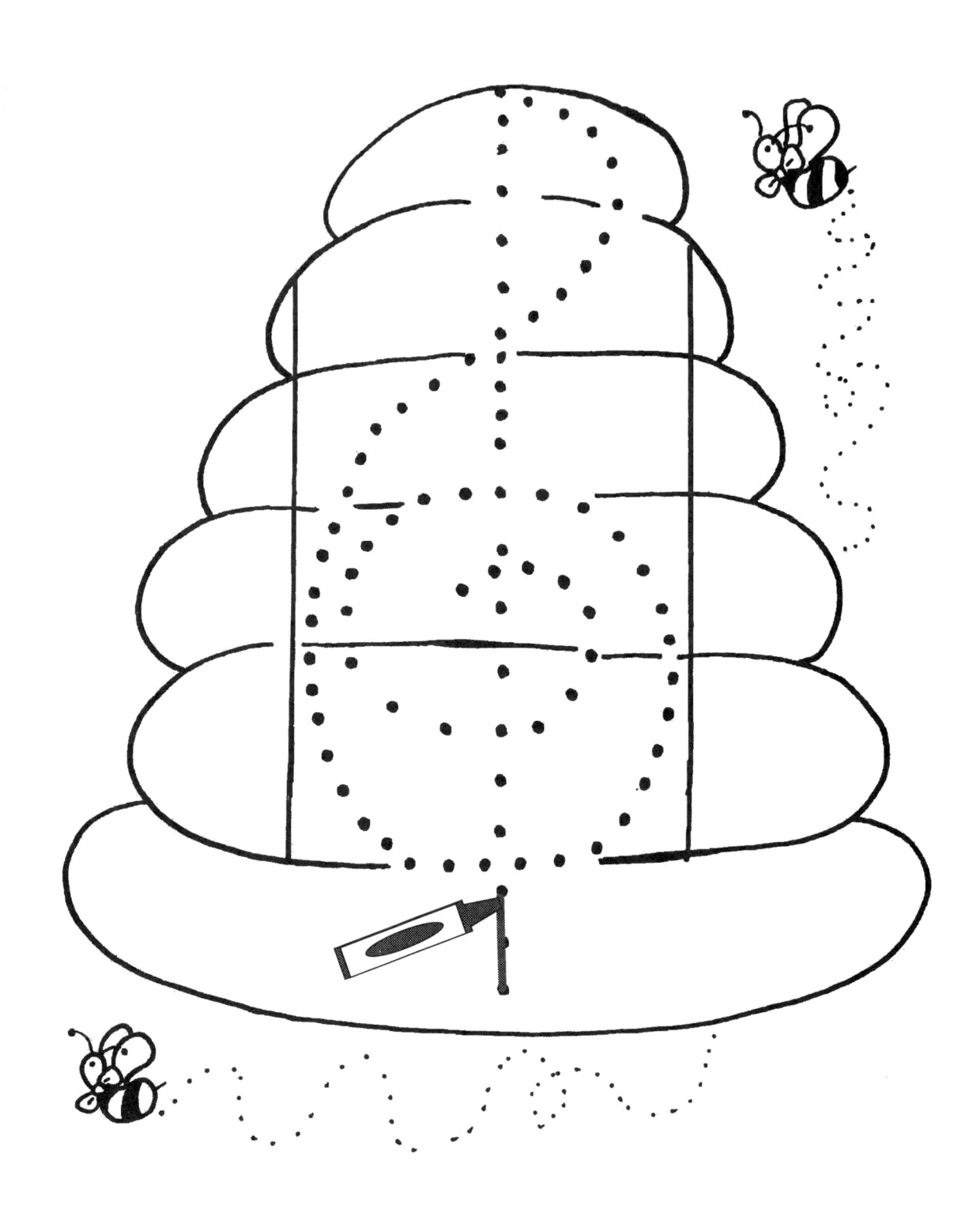

Trace Buzzy Bee's treble clef.

Color things God made high and low.

Color Joash's building site.

# Color the children who are singing while they play.

# Color the picture and build a house with your blocks.